THE FIDDLETOWN JOURNAL

STORIES OF
THE MOTHER LODE

BY EDWARD L. ALLUM

Robert D. Reed Publishers • San Francisco, California

Robert D. Reed Publishers
750 La Playa Street, Suite 647
San Francisco, CA 94121
Phone: (650) 994-6570 • Fax: (650) 994-6579
E-mail: 4bobreed@msn.com
http://www.rdrpublishers.com

Book Designer: Katherine Hyde
Editor: Katherine Hyde
Cover Designer: Julia A. Gaskill at Graphics Plus

ISBN 1-885003-72-2

Library of Congress No. 00-109044

Produced and Printed in the United States of America

To my wife,
who has stood beside me for thirty-one years
and encouraged me to reach for my goals
and to be my own man

ACKNOWLEDGMENTS

I want to thank the partners of the C.S.O. for their friendship and for allowing me to share our stories of the Mother Lode in our search for gold.

I'd like to thank my sister for her constant support throughout my life and the role she plays in our family.

Also, my thanks to the publisher, Robert D. Reed, for his willingness to publish this work and all his valuable efforts in helping make this book a success.

TABLE OF CONTENTS

CHAPTER I

C.S.O., INC.

You won't find C.S.O., Inc., listed in the business section of your daily paper, nor will you find its stock symbol in the quick-quote search on your favorite web page. In this new age of IPOs and fast cash, day traders and triple-digit returns on your investments, this emerging firm is growing based on traditional values, hard work, and the common vision of its work force.

C.S.O., Inc., is totally owned and operated by its employees. Business decisions are based on the 150-year history of the Mother Lode and are as "good as gold."

C.S.O., Inc., was founded in French Camp, in the Central Valley of California, which supplied the Mother Lode camps with food, mining equipment, and a labor force during the great Gold Rush of 1849. Each miner was hell-bent on hitting the pay dirt or lode that would make him rich—the vein that would allow him the comforts and luxuries of living in San Francisco, Reno, Virginia City, or Las Vegas. There food, entertainment, gambling, and the company of beautiful women were abundant, but dependent on the weight of the gold pouch tied to the miner's belt.

The C.S.O., Inc., Board of Directors is made up of a small but dedicated group of miners. The Chairman of the Board and Chief Executive is a miner known only as "Asshole." Most corporations have a CEO or CAO, but we have a CEA, Chief Executive Asshole. His knowledge and experience as a miner and his leadership skills are unsurpassed. He has a remarkable ability to raise working capital; for example, he can crush the beer cans after the board meetings and resell the aluminum for a dollar a pound, where most firms can only realize 94 cents.

There are two senior vice presidents, a.k.a. "Wigwam" and "River Rat." Wigwam is a miner who got his name from his compulsion to gamble at the local Indian casino—only if he couldn't get to Reno, Vegas, Tahoe, Virginia City, or any other place where the one-armed bandits are found and the prime rib of beef is thick and rare.

River Rat is the technological miner who surprises the team with new mining gadgets and aids, like pocket-sized fold-up shovels and telescoping chairs. He favors metal detectors, and also suffers a strong pull to the nightlife, lights, and one-armed bandits found just an hour away in our beloved Nevada.

There are two junior vice presidents, a.k.a. "Grizzly" and "Sourdough." Grizzly is a miner and our firm's chief engineer and equipment operations officer. It is his responsibility to make sure the mining equipment, such as the dredge, pumps, and motors, is fully operational and ready for maximum efficiency. Grizzly, like the bear, tears into the woods and streams with a ferocious unstoppable desire to amass wealth, so he can retire in Minden, Nevada, where he can enjoy the nightlife and fishing on a full-time basis. It should be noted that Mrs. Grizzly does not want to live in Nevada. So we will just have to see who the best bear is.

Sourdough is the newest full-time miner. The management team originally dubbed him "Old Woman," due to his constant whining about the lack of progress of the company, and the risk capital it required to join. He soon relented when he found out there is always cold beer in the corporate cooler.

The final two miners are associate members, a.k.a. "Wimpy" and "Pack Mule." Wimpy is a part-time miner. He is finishing his last year of college and working part-time. He got his name because he always orders a cheeseburger and fries for breakfast at 5:30 A.M., and because he has no resources. Like the cartoon character, he will gladly pay you Tuesday for a hamburger today.

Pack Mule is a fair-weather miner who prefers the special outings, where the ladies are wined and dined in Nevada. He is also known as "Mr. G.Q.," for his impeccable taste in clothes and for the hours he spends primping prior to the festivities. Pack Mule is a first-generation American Chinese, a Berkeley grad and professional. We like to take him along because we feel it is good for him to experience the harsh life of his forefathers, and he is always lucky at the tables and with the ladies.

Now that you have gotten to know us, the following journal entries will allow you the opportunity to experience firsthand the inside workings of C.S.O., Inc., from the weekly board meetings, where strategic planning, policies, and procedures are formulated, to actual scouting trips, mining adventures, and real-life experiences.

Some of these episodes will be too intense for the weak at heart, like hanging off 5,000-foot cliffs at Candy Rock high in the Sierra Mountain ranges, or the whitewater river where some miners floating the dredging equipment downriver almost lost their lives to the water and rocks in our quest for the gold.

CHAPTER II

THE MINER'S
TEN COMMANDMENTS
PLUS TWO

Asshole and Wigwam were the two founding fathers of C.S.O., Inc., and agreed long before the actual incorporation and installation of other members that certain rules and by-laws must be adopted.

Nobody likes rules; however, if one is to be a real gold prospector, some rules just have to be followed. As a baseline, Asshole and Wigwam adopted "The Miner's Ten Commandments," written during the Gold Rush by J. M. Hutchings and reprinted in a book by James Klein, *Where to Find Gold in the Mother Lode* (published by Keen Engineering Co., Northridge, California).

The original Miner's Ten Commandments were written in Old English, so we have adapted these for today's use. The additional two commandments were added to keep the miners' physical exertion to a minimum and their thoughts focused on the task at hand.

➪ You shall work only one claim.

➪ You shall not jump any other man's claim.

➪ You shall not look for a new claim until the old one is tapped, neither shall you take your gold dust to the gaming tables in vain.

➪ You shall not dig or pick on the Sabbath day.

➪ You shall not dwell on thinking of the gold and how you're going to spend it.

➪ You shall not kill yourself by working in the rain, nor kill your neighbor in a duel, nor get tight or stewed while panning.

➪ You shall not grow discouraged, or think of going home.

➪ You shall not steal a pick or a pan or a shovel from your fellow miner, nor take his tools without his leave.

➪ You shall not tell any false tale about good diggings in the mountains.

➪ You shall not commit unsuitable matrimony.

➪ You shall find a river close enough to the road so you may pan from the front seat of your Cadillac.

➪ You shall not talk about your day job while gold panning, or your fellow miners will piss on you in the river.

C.S.O., Inc., has no other written rules. We do discuss all potential mining locations, trips, equipment purchases, and any other business that may come before the board at our Wednesday meetings. A simple majority vote carries the motion.

CHAPTER III

FRENCH CAMP

F rench Camp, California, was settled in the mid-1840s by French miners and was one of the first settlements in San Joaquin County. French Camp is about three miles south of Stockton, the county seat, which is now home to over 250,000 people.

During the Gold Rush, Stockton became the winter home to many of the miners. It also became a melting pot for the immigrants who came either for the gold as prospectors, or as forced laborers. These laborers were put to work either in the mines, or in carving out the mountains for the route of the Great Pacific Trans-Continental Railroad. With the massive and almost immediate growth in population came many new diseases, such as tuberculosis (TB). The founding fathers of Stockton, concerned about the potential spread of TB, decided to build a hospital in French Camp, as the prevailing delta breezes would keep this airborne threat at least three miles south of town. San Joaquin General Hospital (SJGH) was the result of that decision. Now standing for over 150 years, SJGH has served the community well, and will continue to do so well into the new millennium.

I tell you this because SJGH was the center and birthplace of C.S.O., Inc. The majority of the C.S.O. miners worked together there and developed long-lasting friendships and respect for each other.

Asshole (now retired) was a diagnostic imaging (X-ray) film processor with over thirty years with the company. Grizzly (now retired) was the facility manager and chief engineer. He too had over thirty years service with SJGH. River Rat is the current director of materials management. Sourdough is the support services manager for San Joaquin County. Pack Mule is the director of nutrition. Wigwam (now retired) was a deputy director of SJGH, then came out of retirement to be the director of purchasing and support services for San Joaquin County; he recently re-retired.

The C.S.O. was founded around the ashtray outside the hospital, where neither rain, nor bitter cold, nor intense heat could keep the miners from meeting at what became known as "Bob break," to smoke our vile cigarettes. First it was Asshole and Wigwam; then River Rat and Pack Mule joined, followed by Grizzly. Every day we would learn more about each other and our mutual interests. At the ashtray titles, nametags, and corporate status disintegrated as we discussed gold mining and planned our first trip.

Eventually the discussions became the first of our weekly board meetings. We would decide a date when we could all go on an expedition, where we would meet that morning, what river we would conquer, who would drive, and what equipment would be needed to sample the river for a spot of color. So as not to waste the day, our first commitment was to get an early start; the early bird gets the worm. We would meet for breakfast, a hearty meal that would carry us through the day. That usually meant getting our morning chow at the Lockford Inn.

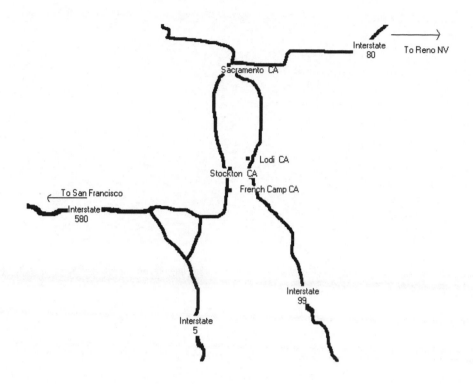

Interstate
80   To Reno NV

Sacramento CA

Lodi CA

Stockton CA

French Camp CA

To San Francisco
Interstate
580

Interstate
99

Interstate
5

Map 1. French Camp

CHAPTER IV

GEORGE'S LOCKFORD INN

In the early days of the C.S.O., the miners agreed to meet at a central location, Lodi, California. Lodi is home to one miner, while others had to come from Stockton or from as far south as Escalon.

Lodi is on the way to Highway 49, the original route of the 49ers and the main highway through the Mother Lode. Our team had to get up as early as four A.M. to gather all the miners for the trip. Once assembled, the caravan would head for George's Lockford Inn, Lockford being the first of the foothill communities.

George, a Greek who has built up a terrific restaurant, owns the Lockford Inn. Not only is the food great, but the service is fast and friendly, and the breakfast specials are more than most miners can handle, complete with sourdough biscuits and breads. The price is more than reasonable and they have a bar too! They open at 5:30 A.M., which is perfect for the team.

Asshole usually orders a Bloody Mary and a short stack of pancakes, while the rest of the team orders a more traditional bill of fare. The miners take turns picking up the bill for the team, rotating every trip. With a good solid breakfast and a lot of bullshit, insults, and lies behind us, we are generally packed up and on the road by 6:15.

Like the miners before us, we are heading into the hills before the sun rises to dig out and pan our pieces of the gold, never knowing what Mother Nature, the woods, the river, or the mountains have planned for us.

CHAPTER V

VALLEY SPRINGS "THE SECRET PLACE"

V alley Springs, California, is located in Calaveras County, on Highway 12 between the towns of Clements and San Andreas. There you'll find some Bureau of Land Management land, open to the public for hand panning (but not for dredging, because it's below Highway 49). This is our secret place—guaranteed gold with easy access. It can be seen to the right of the road and really has two spots. First is the small creek that runs through the cow pasture, and when that's dried up, you can move back down the trail to the more open Calaveras River.

Asshole and Wigwam planned this trip around the ashtray at the hospital, before the days of the C.S.O. Others would hear Asshole talk about the gold. He even had some to show off, so Asshole, Wigwam, Wimpy, and one of the security officers made this first trip. We made arrangements to meet in Lodi and then stopped in Lockford for breakfast.

We arrived at our secret spot just about daybreak, gathered our buckets, pans, shovels, and cooler, and headed for the stream. As the sun rose over the valley, the sunlight started to sparkle on the river; with the sun came the sounds of birds and the tranquil sound of the water trickling over the river rock and our own boots. Each miner distanced himself from the others, just far enough to enjoy his own space, but not to feel all alone.

Now you're away from the phone calls, voice mail, e-mail, and those constant demands for your time, such as that urgent memo calling for your immediate action because the author just left for vacation.

Now it's just you, the river, and your pan. First you place your pan down in the water, cover it with the larger classifier pan (you know, the big one with all the holes drilled in it), then take your shovel and dig up some river bed and fill the classifier pan with dirt, sand, and rock. Then, grabbing both pans, let the river wash over the pans while moving them in a circular motion. The idea is to let the fine gold and black sand sieve through to the bottom pan. Before you throw back the larger rocks from the classifier pan, be sure to look at them, for you may find some gold nuggets or quartz rock with small gold veins running through it.

Now take your small hand pan with your concentrates, and start washing it in a circular motion in the water. You must remember that gold is ten times heavier than water, so you're trying to wash the gold to the bottom of your pan. Your next step is to place your pan on an angle. With the top of the pan at one o'clock and the bottom edge at seven o'clock, gently let the water in the pan wash over your concentrate, working out the small rock, washing down to black sand. On most pans there are ribs formed in the rim; these are called Chinese ribs, as the Chinese invented them. These ribs help to trap the gold in the pan while you are washing out the dirt.

By now you're down to the black sand. Get just enough water in your pan to barely cover the bottom. Looking very closely, tap the side of the pan and use the water to separate the black sand from the gold. Now that the gold flakes are in the bottom corner of your pan, take the sucker bottle and suck up those babies. Another method is to use the dry tip of your finger and press down on the gold, which will stick to your finger. Then place the gold in a sample vial full of water and place the cap back on. Warning: Use a plastic vial so that if you drop it, it won't break when it hits the rocks, because then you have lost your gold.

Sometimes when you get to the bottom of your pan you may find some fool's gold; or if you're like Wigwam, you bottle up anything that shines, just to be safe. He even kept some BBs once, 'cause that's all he found that day. Sometimes you'll find gemstones, like garnets or diamonds, and other times your pan will give you nothing but the reflection of your own face.

Sometimes you may come across some wildlife. You must always keep one eye open for rattlesnakes anytime you are in the mountains. The rattlers like to come out and bask in the early sun. You may also see mountain lions, but the bears are a little higher up the mountain.

It's that simple: you are now a miner, a gold prospector, a mountain man, a dreamer, and part of the history of the Gold Rush and of California.

CHAPTER VI

COLOMA

T he next big trip was set for Coloma, California. Coloma is located in El Dorado County, just above Highway 49, at an altitude of about 3,500 feet. This is not far from the original site
where Marshall found gold, which started the Gold Rush.

Asshole, Wigwam, Wimpy, and about eight others from the hospital (again before the C.S.O. began) put together an expedition to
Coloma. One of the social workers, Tom, owned eighty acres with a
stream, and he said, "Go for it." By the way, Tom trained tigers for a
living while working his way through college for his master's degree.
Tom assured us that all his tigers were at home and not to worry
about them.

So three trucks and one Cadillac met up in Lodi to start the trek
to Coloma. We skipped breakfast this time; Wigwam had some pull
in the hospital kitchen, so he had them make up a dozen super sub
sandwiches, sodas, and chips for the gang. Asshole only wanted
meat and cheese on a dry sub bun, "no fixin's." By now, you must
know why we call him Asshole. We paid the kitchen their customary

fees. Nothing for free in this day of HMOs, PPOs & Preferred Providers—nothing except the gold.

Once we reached the property in Coloma, we unpacked the vehicles, but we could not see the river. We could hear it, but not see it. Someone thought it was just down the side of an embankment a little bit, so Wigwam decided to go first. About five steps down, he lost his balance and down he went. Wigwam weighs over 300 pounds, so when he fell, he started rolling. Some 20 or 25 feet later, he stood up, took one step and fell again, rolling like a cartwheeling jelly doughnut. He finally landed within 150 feet of the river. The rest of the miners made it down the ravine without incident, but the worst was yet to come.

The stream was gorgeous. In most spots, the river was less than 10 to 15 feet wide. It was quiet in some places, and small rapids crossed in other areas. There was even a small waterfall that cascaded into the stream. The trees on the banks were so old and heavy with foliage that they touched each other at the center of the river, spanning the water like a covered bridge and keeping us cool while we panned, but letting in just enough sun to allow us to see.

The miners spread out up and down the river. Some set up their sluice boxes; others got out their six-hundred-dollar metal detectors, while most miners panned the traditional way, by hand. Asshole wanted to make sure Wimpy was awake, so when Wimpy wasn't looking he laced his pan with fake nuggets. A few minutes later, Wimpy started hollering, "I found gold!" over and over again. He soon started to rub it in that the rest of us had not been so lucky, and he was the only true miner in the bunch.

By now it was noon and we were starting to get a little hungry, so we sent Wimpy and another miner back to get the subs, sodas, and beer. It seemed to take them a while, but the food finally got back to us. Lunch was great alongside the quiet little stream. Wimpy started in on his gold find, and I finally told him what Asshole had done. We all had a good laugh, and went back to mining.

There is one thing about mining: as the day goes on, so does the sun. The heat can get to 100, 102, 104 degrees between two and four P.M., so we always like to break out of the stream by one o'clock.

We gathered our tools and made sure that the woods were left as we found them. We started back to the cars.

We had walked about a hundred feet from the river when we realized that Wigwam had actually rolled down a thousand-foot ravine, so steep that we had to traverse it to get back up to the top. The steepness of the hike, along with the 3,500-foot altitude, started to get to Asshole and Wigwam. After the younger miners passed them by, they came back down to help them with their tools and packs. Asshole and Wigwam had to stop about every twenty feet or so to catch their breath and rest for the next traverse. It took a good forty-five minutes for the two to make it to the top of the hill. After they caught their breath, they had a beer and made for the group. They vowed never to get in that situation again: no more ravines. The two resolved only to pan in rivers where the Cadillac could pull up to the riverside and panning could be done from the car.

Unfortunately, there was no major gold find that day—maybe only one flake, if that—but it was a great day, the best.

CHAPTER VII

THE JACKSON RANCHERIA

The town of Jackson is located in the foothills of Amador County, at the junction of Highway 88 and Highway 49. Jackson has a lot of history behind it. It was home to two major mines: the Argonaut mine, claimed during the Gold Rush, then later in the early 1900s the Kennedy mine. They say over $150 million in gold came from these mining operations. Jackson became a typical mining town, with streets lined on both sides with saloons and brothels. Oh—and supplies, too! Jackson was just the place for the hard-working miner to have some fun, let off a little steam, and fuel up with a good steak, or a Chinese dinner at Sammie's. Sammie's is still in operation and still serves a great meal.

As has been the case in so much of America's history, the Indians of the area were forgotten. There are still small communities of Indians from the Miwok tribe scattered throughout the Mother Lode region.

The tribe in Jackson opened up a bingo hall (I'm not sure just when), then added video gaming. Wigwam and his wife have been going out to the Jackson Rancheria, as it has been named, since 1987; it is only 31.6 miles from Lodi and makes a nice day trip. The Rancheria was a small casino, built in a pole-barn style, with a bingo room, a poker room, blackjack tables, a coffee shop, and about 360 video slot machines, keno, fruit, 777, and cherry machines. Smoking was allowed, and drinks were free (sodas, no alcohol). What more could you ask for?

Over the past fifteen years the Rancheria has done so well, they have just completed a $15 million expansion, which includes a hotel, dinner house, live headliner entertainment, and over a thousand new machines. The Rancheria has become a major employer in Amador County—a great place to visit when time does not permit you to travel to the Silver State.

There is one other Indian casino, called the Chicken Ranch, located in Sonora, towards the southern stretch of Highway 49. The C.S.O. miners have adopted both the Chicken Ranch and the Jackson Rancheria as respites at the end of the day's hard work, hot sun, and sometimes sparse production of gold. There is always a chance for the big win and salvation from the lack of color in our pans. Sometimes we win, and sometimes we lose. The green stuff you can always replace from your day job. But for sure we always have fun!

It seems to be a natural fit: the mountains and foothills, the rivers and streams, the day's digging and picking and panning out of your concentrates, the trip into the old historic town, and the final stop at the saloon and casino to maybe win a little at the tables or pull a handle once or twice, to converse with your fellow miners about the day's finds and promises of tomorrow's search; it all just seems so natural. It was the way of the miners before us and demands our respect.

These old-timers were a rare breed. Many had to hike miles back into the woods, up and down ravines and canyons thousands of feet deep, packing in their tools and supplies, as mules were too expensive till you built up a stake. They would dig and pick and pan from sunup till sundown—that's twelve to fifteen hours of sunlight a day in California, in temperatures that surpassed 100 degrees on a regular basis. At the end of the day the miner would take a look at his gold pouch. On a good day it might contain a nugget or two, or maybe just some fine placer gold, but more often it was empty. The miners slept on the riverbank and existed on sourdough and jerky. They awoke in the morning ready to start another day with optimism, faith, and a belief in themselves, that they would find the pay dirt that would lead to the "color."

There has never been a time, while out on an expedition with the C.S.O. panning for gold, that I have not been reminded of the harshness of their lives and the intestinal fortitude it took for these men to live and to survive their daily battle with nature. They have not only my respect, but also my admiration.

CHAPTER VIII

RIVER RAT & PACK MULE

R iver Rat came to work at the hospital in December 1997, just after the gold-panning season was over. He lived in Turlock, California, about forty-five minutes south of French Camp. He was a smoker like Wigwam and Asshole, and soon found his way to the ashtray. We soon found out that River Rat liked the outdoors, fishing, golfing, and football, and after a couple of weeks he was invited to come along and try out mining.

As River Rat lived in Turlock, Wigwam had him spend a Friday night at his place in Lodi, to save him the extra driving. We had a good night with pizza and beer—an early night, 'cause four A.M. comes pretty early.

This was also the first trip for Pack Mule, so Pack Mule, Asshole, and one of the security guards from the hospital all met up in Lodi, then started off to the Lockford Inn for some quick chow.

Asshole and Wigwam decided that as we had some rookies along we should go to Valley Springs. River Rat volunteered to drive, as he had a Jeep Cherokee and we could all fit in one car. With Pack Mule along, we all had to take turns pointing out the local points of interest, like, look, that's what a cow looks like, and the squirrels, etc.— all the things Mr. GQ wasn't accustomed to. He only knows the animals he has seen in the zoo!

Of special interest were the Chinese walls. During the Gold Rush and the building of the railroad, many Chinese were encouraged to come to America to help with these monumental tasks. All through the Mother Lode region you will find these small stone fences, about two feet high, mortared together with just mud. The Chinese were used to clear the land and they made fences with the rock. They say that many of the Chinese would hide their pay and other valuables in the rocks, so they could pick them up later on their way out of the area. Unfortunately, many of them never came home. Hundreds of Chinese men died while blasting out the mountains for gold mines and the railroad. When the work was done, the Chinese that had served so well were driven out of the country by forced deportation. That was America's thank-you for a job well done.

Nowadays, miners with metal detectors walk the fences looking for the Chinese miners' stash of gold and other stuff, and they are still finding it. Now when you visit, in just about every gold mining town you will find a display honoring the Chinese for their contribution to the development of California. A little too late, but it's a start.

Once we reached the BLM land, we all gathered our tools and headed for the stream. There was not a whole lot of water in the stream, but enough to pan. That's when we first noticed that River Rat was Mr. Tech. He brought with him a telescoping chair and a fold-up shovel. He put on some shorts and sandals, set it all up in the river, and sat down with a beer. It was like he was waiting for the nuggets to roll into the pan. It was then that Asshole and Wigwam realized they had a new partner.

River Rat was convinced that there had to be a better way, and Pack Mule was giving it his best shot. Wigwam only found some BBs, but he kept them anyway. Asshole went to the side of the river and did a little high banking. He got a little color, so the day was not lost.

As the day progressed and got a little hotter, we decided to head for the Rancheria, where a miner could cool down and maybe win a little cash. River Rat and Pack Mule won about fifty bucks each at the blackjack tables, and Asshole won about twelve dollars on poker. Wigwam lost his ass as usual, but nothing ventured, nothing gained.

In the following weeks around the ashtray, River Rat, Wigwam, and Asshole decided to form a partnership to explore opportunities to dig for more gold, with less effort.

Twice a day at "Bob break," the three of us would talk only of gold and how to master the mining of it. After a few weeks we agreed that we needed a dredge. The big problem was that complete dredging units—including dredge, pontoons, sluice box, hoses, and permits—would cost a fortune: at minimum three thousand dollars. We decided to pool our money and build one for less.

Asshole started to look in catalogs for dredge motors and pumps big enough to do the job, but light enough to move in the rivers. We found what we needed, but it cost about eight hundred bucks. Wigwam suggested that we call the chief engineer and get his opinion on (1) will it work, and (2) can he get it cheaper through the hospital. Grizzly's answer was yes on both questions. So Grizzly ordered the motor and pump and twenty feet of hose, and we got it for under six hundred bucks.

Asshole picked up the motor and built a PVC pipe frame to mount it to. Now we had to figure out how we were going to float it. River Rat donated a beach-type multicolored inner tube, and with some bungee cords to strap it down, we had our dredge.

Asshole mailed away for the state dredging permit (thirty-four bucks) and we were ready. So for about six hundred and fifty bucks we now had a dredge. As long as the inner tube had air, it should float! We were ready for the next trip.

CHAPTER IX

GRIZZLY

Grizzly was the facility manager and chief engineer for the hospital, and as such had daily contact with Wigwam. Wigwam would call Grizzly every morning to see how he was and discuss various hospital issues. Mostly Wigwam just wanted to shoot the breeze, as he respected Grizzly and looked to him for guidance.

Grizzly was instrumental in helping us pick out the dredge and save some bucks. One morning he asked, "Do you really find gold? Can I come along?" and "What the hell are you guys going to do with the equipment?" Wigwam invited Grizzly to come on down to the ashtray for "Bob break," and he could decide if he wanted to come along. Grizzly started showing up for our meetings and soon decided he would like to come along and give it a try.

After a couple of days, it dawned on us that if River Rat couldn't come one day, we would have no way to transport the dredge. The group decided to look for a small trailer that could be used to transport the dredge and other equipment. River Rat found an ad in the Lodi news, and the group sent him and Grizzly to look at it. Remember, River Rat was the purchasing agent, and Grizzly the engineer.

They could inspect the trailer and negotiate the best purchase price. The seller wanted two hundred bucks, but through tough negotiation they got him to come down to one hundred seventy-five.

Asshole, River Rat, and Wigwam decided that Grizzly had contributed much to the partnership already and the man hadn't even gotten a shovel wet yet. We voted and told Grizzly if he wanted to be a full partner, we had voted him in. We decided that two hundred dollars was one-fourth of the total investment, and Grizzly bought in. The C.S.O. was now firmly established: four guys that got along and worked and played well together.

Asshole gave our new partner his miner's name, Grizzly Old Fart. Grizzly had been stereotyped around the hospital as gruff, and had a tendency to speak his mind, no matter about what or to whom he was speaking. Soon after, Grizzly protested the "Old Fart" part of his name, and we agreed, because once you got to know him he was more like a teddy bear.

The partners, along with their new trailer and dredging unit, were now ready to attack the wilderness with all the latest mining equipment and technology available. Asshole had even found a metal detector at a flea market. He bought some batteries and we were ready for Fiddletown.

CHAPTER X

FIDDLETOWN

Fiddletown is located just past Jackson, off Highway 49 before you get to Plymouth. Fiddletown has only a few of the original buildings that stood during the rush. It got its name because the miners of the time found only small amounts of placer gold, and really spent most of their time just fiddling around. So why did we go there?

Asshole worked in the X-ray department, and one of the ladies who worked there told him about her property. She said that her father used to pan there. It was private property, with a river running through it, a runoff of the Consumnes River, so why not give it a try? The partners agreed, so we were off.

Grizzly, coming from Escalon, picked up Asshole in Stockton at four A.M. They loaded up the trailer with the dredge, tools, and beer and headed for Lodi. River Rat drove from Stockton out to Wigwam's to pick him and Wimpy up. Once everyone was on board we headed off to Lockford for breakfast and then headed out on the road.

Asshole had the map drawn on a piece of paper and was in the lead car. We have since learned not to let Asshole read the map 'cause he always screws it up. After some reorganization, we found the property. The owner knew we were coming, so she had placed a sign on the road and had even cut down the brush to make a car parking lot as close as she could to the river. It was trucks only beyond that point.

Once at the river's edge, River Rat, Mr. Tech, started to blow up the inner tube with a compressor attached to the lighter in his jeep. We strapped the dredge to the tube and launched the unit.

Asshole had the state permit and was going to have to do the dredge sucking. He started to put on his wetsuit—the yellow one that makes him look like a banana. The top and neckpiece must have been too tight, 'cause Asshole couldn't breathe and his face was turning blue. Wigwam pulled out his knife and put it to Asshole's throat and cut away some of the rubber so he could breathe. After Asshole threw up, he was okay. We never knew if it was the suit, or the Bloody Mary and pancakes, or just excitement, but he was okay.

The dredge now launched and Asshole in the water, we started up the dredge, and it worked just like the store-bought manufactured ones. This was a great success for the partners, and gave us a lot of encouragement. While Asshole and Grizzly ran the dredge, River Rat, Wimpy and Wigwam hand-panned and sampled for color. Wigwam and Wimpy started to find gold right away; over fifteen good-sized flakes were accumulated in the course of the morning.

After three hours of operation, we called it quits. With the sluice box we had collected a five-gallon pail of concentrate to take back and hand-pan out during the week. The only major problem was that the beach-type tire could not hold enough air to keep the rig stable. Grizzly said he would pick up a tractor-trailer tube for the next outing.

The very next week, Asshole was walking across the hospital campus and stepped in a hole, blowing out his knee. The partners were all concerned, as Asshole had the only dredging permit. The rest of the season was up in the air.

On our last trip to Fiddletown, Asshole was laid up, but he went anyway, sitting on the riverbank with beer in hand and shouting orders like a general or a mother hen, I don't know which. Grizzly brought his swimsuit so he could do the dredge vacuuming. With the new tire tube under the rig, Grizzly sat in the river, dredge hose in one hand and beer in the other, with a smile on his face from ear to ear. I was having trouble deciding whether he looked more like Homer Simpson or Yogi the Bear; I think the bear.

River Rat, Wigwam and Wimpy continued to hand-pan and helped to shovel bedrock in the direction of Grizzly and the dredge vacuum, until we packed up for the day.

After three trips to Fiddletown, the partners only got a little gold, not much more than we found on the first trip. This was disappointing, because it was now October and dredging season was over. But we were able to test the equipment and make necessary improvements after each trip. We also got to know each other even better, and with each trip we became even better miners.

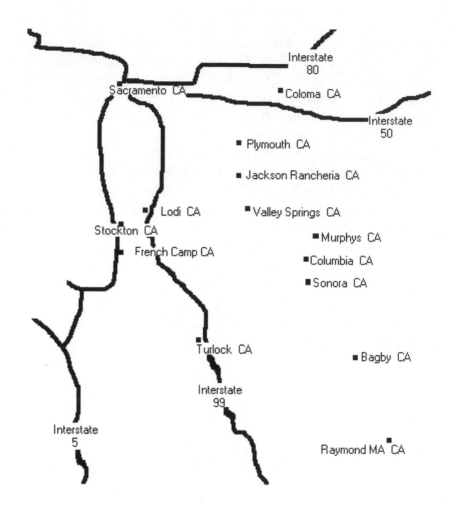

Interstate 80

Coloma CA

Sacramento CA

Interstate 50

Plymouth CA

Jackson Rancheria CA

Lodi CA

Valley Springs CA

Stockton CA

Murphys CA

French Camp CA

Columbia CA

Sonora CA

Turlock CA

Bagby CA

Interstate 99

Interstate 5

Raymond MA CA

Map 2. Fiddletown

CHAPTER XI

THE GOLD FAIRY

D redging season was now over, but the partners agreed to continue to meet at least once a month for breakfast or lunch, just to keep it all going and see how we were all doing. Wigwam called all the partners, including Pack Mule and Wimpy, and said we needed to meet at On Loc Sam's in Stockton for lunch. Sam's is another Chinese place that has been around for over a hundred years. We agreed on a time and had a great lunch.

The Gold Fairy had six boxes that were to be handed out to the miners after lunch. One box was given to each miner, with only a note, "From the Gold Fairy." The Gold Fairy had gotten each of the miners matching knives from the Franklin Mint. The knives were part of a special limited edition, commemorating 150 years since the Gold Rush.

Each knife was trimmed in gold and silver and had a miniature gold coin mounted in the handle, with a picture of a miner panning in the river. I think the miners were surprised and really liked them. For me, I felt that the knives represented all that we had been through together, our struggle and our connection to the past.

CHAPTER XII

LAKE TOPAZ EXPEDITION

By now winter had set into the Sierras and mining was at a standstill. Winter in the Sierras can be brutal. You've all read or heard stories of the Donner Party, who starved and re-sorted to cannibalism while trying to get across the Sierras in the winter of 1846–7. To this day, many of the mountain passes are just plain locked up and closed to the public till spring. Only Highway 80 to Reno and Highway 50 to Tahoe are kept open most of the year. But they, too, find themselves closed when the big storms hit.

With a long winter ahead, the partners decided that we would plan a spring fishing trip for early April. We found out that Lake Topaz is located just south of Minden, Nevada, on Highway 395: a nice fishing lake with small cabins. They rent fishing boats, and gee, they have a casino too.

Wigwam was asked to organize the trip, so he developed a survey of potential dates, and asked questions like, "Would you like to drive? Smoking or nonsmoking? Share a room or have your own?" etc. After word got out around the hospital, over fourteen people responded to the survey. But as the time grew close, only the partners and Pack Mule, plus one other, agreed to go.

The date was set, April 4. Wigwam made all the reservations for rooms and boats. We agreed to meet at Wigwam's, head to Lockford for breakfast and then up the hill 150 miles to Lake Topaz. Just like a regular outing.

One problem, Grizzly lived in Escalon and had to pick up Asshole. So Wigwam offered to pick up Asshole and Grizzly at work to spend the night at Wigwam's and leave the next morning, when the rest of the partners showed up.

After work on the eve of the trip, Wigwam picked up the partners and took them to his house in Lodi. They started to have a few beers, which led to a few boilermakers. Wigwam has a small room in his house that he calls "The Saloon." He has a collection of four slot machines plus a jukebox with all the golden oldies and a lot of Motown music, as Wigwam is from Detroit.

By the time Mrs. Wigwam got home from work, Grizzly, Asshole, and Wigwam were plastered beyond help, singing along as a trio to "The Duke of Earl" and other jukebox hits. They were slamming quarters into the slots. Clearly the expedition had already started. Mrs. Wigwam ordered pizza and Asshole paid for it. Wigwam called River Rat and Pack Mule and told them to come on out and get an early start, but they proved to be the wiser of the group and stayed away.

Four A.M. comes pretty damned early when you don't know who the hell you are or what you have been doing. Despite that, we managed to get up, have some black coffee, and wait for the rest of the expedition to show up. Right on time, all were here and it was time to leave for Lockford. Wigwam was still so hammered that he let Grizzly drive the Northstar, as Asshole doesn't drive. Actually Asshole does drive, but not after dark, or in the rain, or in the fog, or if the speed limit is more than 25 miles per hour. So you might as well say he doesn't drive.

When we got to the Lockford Inn, they opened up the doors for us. Asshole ordered his customary Bloody Mary and Wigwam had to be escorted to the table. Wigwam forgot to order sausage, so he started to steal it from Pack Mule. The waitress, seeing this, felt sorry for Pack Mule and brought him some more sausage. Remember, the girls like Pack Mule.

Finally, on our way up Highway 88, we passed through Jackson, Pine Grove, Pioneer, Cook's Station, and Ham's Station. Then without warning, a winter storm started and driving became a little tricky. We went on to Peddler's Hill, through Carson Pass to just before Kirkwood, where, at about 8,000 feet, River Rat's jeep took a spin and almost went over the side. At the same time we saw a timber wolf. Everything was downhill from there. On to Picket's Junction, the Nevada state line, Minden, turn right on 395 and head for Gardnerville, and the next stop, Lake Topaz.

Lake Topaz, Nevada, is located in what's called high desert, with temperatures generally in the mid 60s to 70s this time of the year. But not today: 32 degrees, overcast, and no one could take a boat out. So, after checking in, we made the best of a bad situation; we went to the casino.

The machines at the Lake Topaz lodge are the tightest machines we have ever encountered anywhere. Pack Mule did okay at the tables, as usual, but the rest of us were just getting our butts kicked. We all broke for dinner. The steak house was quite nice. Most of us ordered prime rib, and when it came to the table it was about three pounds of steak for each. Wigwam was so sick, he could only eat a few bites of his, but the rest of the guys thought the food was great.

Asshole and Wigwam gave up and went to their rooms about 8:30. The rest of the guys followed much later. Asshole and Wigwam were up the next morning at 4:30 and started calling the rooms to get the others rousted out of bed. We all met for breakfast, then hit the road.

There was only one stop on the way home, at the Indian Smoke Shoppe. All the smokers filled their trunks with cigs—ten bucks per carton cheaper than in California.

The partners agreed that Lake Topaz is permanently off the expedition schedule. We will replace it with Reno or Tahoe.

CHAPTER XIII

BAGBY

Bagby is located in Tuolumne County. Follow Highway 49 till you get to Highway 120, turn and head up the hill towards Yosemite National Park.

After our poor results in Fiddletown, the partners decided that we would try for some color in the southern region of the Mother Lode. Grizzly lived in Escalon, so we decided to meet at his house, have breakfast in Oakdale, and head out for the Merced River. River Rat, Asshole, and Wigwam all met up at the customary four A.M. and headed down to Grizzly's. Asshole rode with Grizzly and the equipment, while River Rat and Wigwam followed in River Rat's jeep.

After breakfast, we headed up the hill. Our first stop was at Priest. We pulled off the road and checked out the river. The span of the river was pretty wide and it just did not have the feel of a good mining site. In fact, I think there was even a boat launch ramp, which as the day progressed would have been inundated with city folks, launching their jet skis and such.

We decided to keep moving up the hill for more suitable digs and less civilization. Grizzly suggested we head up to Bagby and check that out. About an hour later, at about 3,500 feet, we reached Bagby and the Merced River. Our potential spot lay before the dams and right at the river's source.

Bagby is on BLM land that is managed by a private company. They have a real campground and facilities, with restrooms and showers. We stopped the trucks and walked to the river's edge to inspect the area. By now it was eleven o'clock and we would have to drag all the equipment for about a city block, get set up, and maybe get one hour of dredging. A little disappointed, we decided to just take a break and enjoy the mountains. About the time we opened the first beer, up pulls Ranger Jim.

Ranger Jim, complete with a Smokey the Bear hat, was really pleasant. He explained that most of the miners with dredging units go to the end of the park and sign a waiver at the gate, waiving our right to sue in case of injury or death. We had Asshole fill it out because he had the dredge permit. Ranger Jim explained that in this region, dredging units must be made of either plastic or aluminum and must be on pontoons to protect the river. We argued that our truck inner tube was a pontoon, and Ranger Jim said with a wink, "OK this time." He then explained we needed to follow the dirt trail for about five miles back. Ranger Jim wished us well.

The fire road was a typical one-car-wide, winding mountain road that had its ups, downs, and potholes, the kind of road that finds itself at times clinging to the side of the mountain. You have to use the creeper gear. I suppose that's so you can hear the rocks crumble and fall off the side of the mountain a thousand feet to the bottom, where they find their final resting place in the river below, and pray that you won't join them.

After much cussing, bouncing, and white knuckles, we reached the end of the trail, a wide-open space, a perfect space, but the river was still about one-and-a-half miles away. With a four-wheeler you could drive right to the river's edge, but our trucks were only two-wheel drive. Should we risk it?

Due to the time of day and the fear of getting stuck, we agreed to come another day, better prepared. On the way out we noticed that some miners had permanent-type dive stations where the dredge with scuba gear was stored. Maybe someday after we find enough gold, we will be able to afford such equipment.

Heading down the hill and traveling through the mountains, we soon came to Chinese Camp. We had decided to go on to Sonora, just to do some scouting, when Grizzly made a rather abrupt left-hand turn and we were on Chicken Ranch Road.

The Chicken Ranch is the smaller of our two frequented Indian casinos; it has a bingo hall and only about a hundred slot machines. This unplanned stop turned out to be very successful. Wigwam only had twenty dollars on him at the time, which he loaded into what he thought was a quarter machine. When he went to place the bet, he realized it was a dollar machine, and he blurted out some kind of expletive. The bandit had his twenty, so he figured he might as well play. Wigwam bet the eight-dollar maximum and hit six out of nine sevens, which paid him $204. River Rat followed with a win of $180, and Asshole hit for $75. Grizzly was down $50 and was not the happy bear. All this happened in fifteen minutes. We got the hell out of there so we could go home winners.

CHAPTER XIV

LADIES' NIGHT OUT

The partners had been panning and meeting on a pretty regular basis, particularly when you take into account that we also met every Wednesday at Asshole's for our weekly board meetings.

The board met and decided on a strategy to strengthen our position for time off requested for the next gold-panning season. Like all corporations, we felt that we had better recognize the wives and/or significant others with a ladies' night out. This would ensure that we could continue with our mining efforts. This was a wise and calculated move, designed to make sure that the wives didn't think we were having too much fun without them.

Wigwam suggested that we take the ladies for an overnighter to Reno. Yeah, that's the ticket, an evening of fine dining, drink, gambling, headliner entertainment, a hotel suite with hot tub, bar, and sauna. What more could they want? They might even win a little. All corporations have to spend money on political action; some have even made campaign donations in hopes of steering legislation in their favor. This only made good business sense. The board voted: We would buy the wives off with a trip to Reno.

Wigwam was given the duty of booking the rooms at the best possible price, and at the casino that would meet most of the group's needs. The date was set for March 19 (that is usually rainy season and too early to pan or dredge anyway). All was set.

The Peppermill Hotel and Casino is one of Reno's best, with the finest suites and amenities, a newly remodeled and expanded casino floor, fine restaurants, and live entertainment. The ladies should be impressed with this place. Each partner explained in his own special way that this trip was to honor the sacrifices that his lady had made, and this was going to be her night on the town. The sky's the limit.

So the partners agreed to meet up at the Lockford Inn for a 7:30 breakfast. Pack Mule hadn't been able to go panning for a while but did like the idea of the Reno trip. The rest of the partners decided to set him up with the breakfast bill for all thirteen of us. We told him it was his turn. You should have seen his face when we told the waitress, "One check please. Give it to Pack Mule." Needless to say, we all split the bill and had a great breakfast.

Grizzly had a surprise, party favors for each couple (we think Grizzly actually wrapped them himself). To our surprise, we all received a small vial of gold flakes. You know, the kind of bottle that you can pick up in most of the Mother Lode towns, in the souvenir shops.

Off to Reno we go! Like ducks in a row, we headed out from the Lockford Inn and turned right onto Highway 88. Reno, here we come!

An hour and a half later we were in Minden, Nevada, home of the Carson Valley Inn on Highway 395. The Inn is a nice little casino that caters more to the older crowd, you know, the snowbirds, or seniors. We decided to stop and play a little, as we had time to kill. Check-in at the Peppermill was not till one P.M., so we might as well play our way to Reno. After an hour, we actually had all won a little. Grizzly won about $150, Asshole won, and Wigwam was up twelve bucks. We decided to get out while we were ahead and hit the road.

Heading north on 395, we soon got to Carson City, the capital of the Silver State. We pulled off and stopped at the Golden Nugget Saloon and Casino, just to kill a little more time and hopefully pick up some more cash. Did I say pick up some cash?! The Nugget was not as kind as the Carson Valley Inn. Lady Luck must have been out for lunch or in the ladies' room, 'cause we got our asses kicked big time.

We finally made it. The last stop, The Peppermill, a shining jewel in the desert, where the service is unsurpassed, the valet runs up to park your car and the bellman grabs your bags. It's on to check-in and up to the suite. After a little freshening up, it's down to the casino floor, where the lights are bright, the drinks are free, and the machines and tables await you. This is it! Your lucky day; you're going to break the house, you're going to own the place by the end of the night. After a couple of hours you could see the partners lined up at the ATMs restocking their wallets. We'll get them on the next round. Thank God it's time for dinner.

The partners agreed to meet at the steak house for dinner at six o'clock. However, only Mr. & Mrs. Grizzly and Mr. & Mrs. Wigwam showed up. We made the necessary calls to all the rooms, but the rest of the gang were nowhere to be found. So just the four of us had dinner together, a pleasant meal of good food and great conversation. We soon found out it was Mrs. Grizzly's birthday, so that made the meal even a little more special.

We went back to the casino floor to try to recapture our losses. Grizzly and his wife had show tickets, so they were spared some of the financial losses. Play and play and play until you can't take it any more, then up to the room for a hot tub and rest.

The next morning, rested and broke, the partners met up for breakfast and to head down the hill. There is always one rule when you go to Reno: fill your gas tank before you go to the hotel, so at least you can get home. Even if it's only half a tank, you can make it 'cause it's all downhill from there.

At the next board meeting, the consensus was that all of the ladies had a great time. Our plan had worked! We had won them over! And our time off requests for the new panning season were secured.

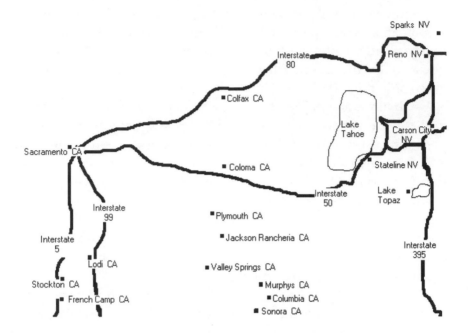

Map 3. Nevada

CHAPTER XV

SOURDOUGH, CHOWCHILLA, & RETIREMENT

G rizzly, Asshole, and Wigwam had been conspiring and making their plans to retire from the hospital as soon as possible. The plan was to get out in September and gold pan as much as we could. Wigwam went first on his birthday in August, and that really pissed off Grizzly and Asshole, 'cause they were both older. But they soon followed, both retiring in September.

Two weeks after Wigwam retired, he got a call from the county administrator, asking, "Can you help us out of a jam?" The county CAO wanted Wigwam to fill an interim position for the county purchasing and support services department. Wigwam had no choice but to say yes, as the position paid well and this would make him a county department head. Grizzly and Asshole really thought that was great 'cause they got to retire six months before Wigwam after all.

Wigwam had a manager who worked with him who also smoked. So around the ashtray outside the courthouse, Wigwam got to be friends with this man. Over the next few weeks, Wigwam started calling him "Old Woman," because he was always whining about something. Old Woman sounded like he would be interested in gold panning, so Wigwam invited him to a couple of board meetings. The C.S.O. board always allows someone to try panning with us one time. Then they have to make up their minds if they want to buy in, and the board decides if we want them.

As this was the off season, Old Woman got to come to several board meetings before he actually went on an expedition. He really didn't like the "Old Woman" thing and asked for a name change. So Asshole named him "Sourdough."

Sourdough's brother Mac happened to own nine acres of land in Madera County, just outside the town of Raymond, north of Highway 49, with the Chowchilla River running straight through it. This area had been a high gold-producing area, so we planned the next trip there.

As Madera is south of Escalon, we all met up at Grizzly's, stopped for breakfast at some Denny's restaurant, and were on the road by 6:30. We got to Mac's place early in the morning and the partners started to set up the dredge. Once it was operational, Sourdough, Wigwam, River Rat, and Wimpy started hand-panning, while Asshole and Grizzly ran the dredge. It was a gorgeous day. Mac and his wife treated us like family.

Down on the river, after we had been mining for some time, Grizzly made a motion that we offer Sourdough a full partnership. It was a unanimous vote and Sourdough was in, if he wanted to come up with the two hundred dollars (his portion of what the corporation had invested to stake the C.S.O.). Sourdough seemed to be a good fit, so we took another vote and lowered his fee to one hundred. The C.S.O. was now five partners strong.

After several hours of mining, we broke up camp. When we went up to Mac's house to say thanks, they had the bar set up with everything anyone could want to drink. And so we did! After several goodbyes, being a little high-spirited, we were on our way back.

About thirty minutes down the road, the caravan pulled over and all the miners were soon standing in an orchard taking leaks. There was a great sense of relief among us all, and we finished the trip without further problems.

CHAPTER XVI

GOLD PROSPECTORS ASSOCIATION OF AMERICA

T he Gold Prospectors Association of America, more commonly known as GPAA, has been around for many years. It offers many benefits and lots of information for its members. For several board meetings Asshole had been suggesting that we split the cost of membership so we could get the map book and a permit to mine the claims that the GPAA owns or leases. This would get us in with the big boys and lead to better gold finds. After some weeks, Wigwam decided to join, as he was still working and could afford the $77 for dues.

The kit arrived: a GPAA hat, a GPAA bumper sticker, a GPAA arm patch, a GPAA gold pan, a GPAA magazine, a GPAA sucker bottle, and most importantly, the GPAA map book and permit to access the lands of the GPAA.

Wigwam gave the hat to Sourdough and took the map book to the next board meeting. The miners were all excited, 'cause this would give us access to places like Italian Bar and other locations that have been touted in their magazine.

To tell the truth, we really were not happy with the map book, 'cause most of the maps were topographical and were difficult to match up with road maps. As Wigwam was from Detroit, he had no clue where anything was anyway. The map book was left for Asshole and Grizzly to interpret and study. By the next board meeting, Asshole and Grizzly had determined that the next trip would be to Italian Bar. We figured, why fool around, we'll just go to the GPAA's premiere spot, pick up the gold, and be back in time for lunch. It sounded like a plan. So we were off!

CHAPTER XVII

COLUMBIA & ITALIAN BAR

T his was the day we were all waiting for, the big expedition to Italian Bar. Italian Bar is located on the southern Stanislaus River, about five miles outside Columbia, just off Highway 49, in Tuolumne County.

Columbia is now a state park. The town has been restored to its Gold Rush glory, complete with horse-drawn buggies, a gold-panning hut for the kids, and gold mine tours. Columbia at one time was one of the largest towns and one of the largest mining operations in California. It's a great place to visit, any time of the year.

As you reach Columbia, you turn down Main Street and it dead-ends at Italian Bar Road; turn left and follow the road for about five miles. Soon the blacktop changes to gravel. Then the road starts to get a little rougher. As you turn the hill, you're now overlooking the ravine—about 2,000 feet down to the river's bottom. A few miles more and you're finally down to the river's edge and what seems to be a great park, with RVs, facilities, etc. An eye-catching sign says, "Welcome to the Lost Dutchman's Mining Association Camp at Italian Bar."

With our GPAA membership card in hand, Asshole went to the manager's office and tried to get some information. He found out the Lost Dutchman's Mining Association owns this claim and it's not open to GPAA members. We can join the LDMA for a mere $3,500 a head. As the miners didn't have $14,000 with them, the office gave us an application. They will even take monthly payments. Gee, that's good to know.

We walked over to the water's edge and watched the raging whitewater pass us by. Wigwam noticed a large rock sticking up from the water with shiny gold stuff in it. He stepped into the river, snatched it up and showed it to the partners. They all said it was fool's gold, but Wigwam didn't care. He stuffed it in his pocket as a souvenir of Italian Bar.

We then asked for directions to the GPAA land and they were nice enough to point back up the hill to where the culvert crosses the road. Still optimistic, we headed back up the hill and sure enough, there was the sign, pointing 900 feet down the side of the hill. This is not a 900-foot walk down the street. This is so steep that it has to be traversed, and it would take several trips to get our gear down. We would never get the dredge down there unless we hired a helicopter. A little pissed off, Asshole, Grizzly, Sourdough and Wigwam headed back to Columbia for a beer in the public parking lot. Wigwam was really mad 'cause he was out $77 for the GPAA membership. Oh well, at least he has another new gold pan.

As we looked at our watches we said, "Now what?" Wigwam said, "Let's go to the Chicken Ranch." But they didn't open till 10:00 A.M., so Wigwam then suggested that we go to the Columbia flea market we had passed on the road. The miners agreed. Maybe we'll find something worth something?

As the miners walked through the flea market, Wigwam spotted some dredging pontoons. They looked good, so he went to find Asshole and Grizzly. We found Sourdough, and decided that we would get them if the price was right. We sent Asshole to negotiate the price. The guy wanted a hundred bucks; we said, "No way." We told Asshole to go back and tell the guy fifty bucks, take it or leave it. He took it.

The partners now loaded their new pontoons up in the truck. This was great 'cause we had just saved about $150; if we bought them new they would be $200. We were happy miners now. With the pontoons we can go on any river at any time. Also, the rest of the partners who could not go on this trip would be happy that we saved some money.

We headed off to the Chicken Ranch to salvage the rest of the day. The Ranch had remodeled since our last visit and the place was quite nice. They must have adjusted the odds on the machines too, to pay for the remodeling, 'cause the partners all lost except Sourdough. He hit for about a hundred dollars.

No gold, no big wins at the Chicken Ranch, but not all was lost. The C.S.O. now had pontoons. We could rid ourselves of the inner tube and be a little more professional.

CHAPTER XVIII

CANDY ROCK

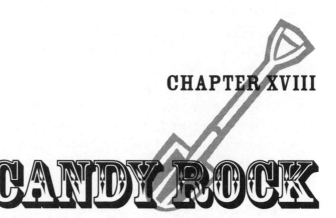

As Grizzly, Asshole and Wigwam were already retired, the rest of the partners decided that we three could take scouting trips to check out a prospective mining site before the whole group wasted a Saturday. It sounded okay with the retirees, so they decided to check out Candy Rock.

Candy Rock is located north of Highway 49, on Highway 4, just beyond Murphy's, in Calaveras County; actually, just past the Big Trees State Park, where the redwoods still grow.

Grizzly and Asshole picked up Wigwam in Lodi and headed to Lockford for some chow. After another great breakfast, we headed up the hill. Past Valley Springs and San Andreas, on to Angels Camp, past Murphy's, two miles past the Big Trees Park to the north dam road; we turned right and started down the road. A short distance down the road, we came upon the dam. We must have taken a wrong turn. There was a worker nearby, so Asshole asked him which way to Candy Rock. "Go back and take the fork to the right." "Okay, thanks a lot."

It started out to be a nice gravel road. The guy said we had to go about 15 miles. We were cutting through the back half of Big Trees Park and the woods were just beautiful. All of a sudden the road turned into a fire road, one lane and full of potholes. Grizzly had his new Ram truck, a gold four-wheeler. He said, "No problem." Wigwam was riding shotgun, with Asshole in the middle.

A few miles more and Grizzly rounded a corner. We were now about 5,000 feet up the mountainside with no guardrails. Wigwam looked out the window and just about threw up. His palms got sweaty and his heart rate was rising. Wigwam yelled, "Stop this GD thing!" Grizzly asked, "What's wrong?" and Wigwam told him to get out and look. We stopped the truck, got out and found we were on the top of the hill. The river was about two miles down this road, if that's what you wanted to call it.

Wigwam said, "Let's turn this thing around and get the hell out of here!" But there was nowhere to turn. We were committed. So Grizzly put the truck in creeper gear and we started down the hill at about three miles per hour. The sides of the truck were barely clearing the sides of the mountain. The road beneath us had washed away in spots and there were no side rails to keep us from falling. We had to listen to the constant sound of rocks spitting out from beneath the tires and slapping their way over the side, hitting other rocks as they descended the mountain. Boy, this really sucked.

Finally, at the bottom, there was a circular drive that headed you back up the hill. We stopped and got out. Damn, not again. We could hear the river but couldn't see it. About another 250 yards down a footpath was the river. The partners just smiled at each other and popped a beer, before we started the trek back up the mountain.

Candy Rock was off the list forever. There was no way we could move operations into this location. It took a good forty-five minutes to get up the hill and back to the main road. Wigwam didn't recover for a long time.

As this was a scouting trip, the partners talked about driving way over to Placer County to check out a spot Sourdough had heard about, but that was another 150 miles. Oh, well, there's always the Rancheria.

As the miners had done so many times before, we pulled into the Rancheria parking lot seeking food and the comforts of the casino. Wigwam pulled up to his favorite machine and hit for $300. Asshole hit for $90 and poor Grizzly was down $57. After about an hour, the miners left, disappointed with the scouting trip, but happy with their winnings. The trip was successful in one sense: all the partners did not waste a valuable Saturday on Candy Rock.

CHAPTER XIX

COLFAX

The miners reported on the scouting trip at the next board meeting. There was some disappointment, but we agreed to do another scouting trip midweek.

Sourdough's neighbor is a miner and told him that we ought to try the Bear River up in Colfax. "If you can't find gold there, you never will." So the retirees agreed to meet up at Wigwam's and take the Cadillac, as this would mostly be highway driving and we might as well be comfortable. As it was a weekday, we wanted an early start to get through Sacramento before the rush hour, so we skipped the Lockford Inn and decided to eat somewhere up the hill.

The miners were having a great time talking and bullshitting about a lot of stuff when Wigwam noticed that they were at Eagles Lake, about five miles from Donner's Pass. We had overshot our exit by about 30 miles. We were closer to Reno than we were to Colfax. We turned around and headed back down Highway 80 to the 174 Junction and got off in Colfax. It was only eight A.M., so we looked for a place to eat.

There was a place called Ed's Little Red Hen restaurant. The menu was written in longhand on the walls. The food was okay, but a little pricey. It was Asshole's turn to buy. After breakfast we headed for Bear River, just about five miles out of town.

We found it. We could drive right up to it. There were campgrounds, facilities, and it was perfect. Wigwam, Grizzly, and Asshole got out their pans and checked for color for about an hour. We then drove to the other end of the park, the end where the dredges and other miners were set up.

We came upon an old-timer who, as we later learned, had been mining there for about twenty-five years. He even had a picture album in his truck of all the gold he had gotten from Bear River over the years. Asshole and Grizzly walked down the river with the old guy to check out the area.

Wigwam called Pack Mule on his cell phone and reported in. "We've found the perfect spot! Pass it on to River Rat." This had been a very successful scouting trip. We left Colfax and the Bear River with great expectations.

We wanted to stop in Auburn on the way back at a place called Pioneer Mining Supplies, operated by Frank and Mindy. Asshole wanted to look at nozzles for the end of the dredge and find out what they did. Grizzly the engineer had already figured it out, but we wanted to stop and check it out anyway. We got a little lost trying to find the place, but with Mindy's help on the cell phone, we finally got there. As we walked in, they were cooking sourdough waffles with rum butter and syrup. We were invited to taste some and they were great.

Grizzly bought a cookbook, and Wigwam bought a small rock pick hammer. Frank explained about the nozzle, so we bought one of those too, for seventy bucks. This would keep the rocks from going through our pump motor, and the C.S.O. company engineer approved. With our mining supplies in hand and some newfound friendships made with Frank and Mindy, we were headed for home, to report the results of our scouting trip at the next board meeting.

CHAPTER XX

THE BEAR RIVER

A t the board meeting the miners received the scouting report with great excitement. It sounded like the ideal spot, and we had confirmed sources that the gold was there for the taking. We agreed that this would be our next expedition.

The miners all agreed to meet up at Denny's Restaurant in Lodi, as it was open at five A.M. and located on Highway 99. It was River Rat's turn to pick up breakfast. Grizzly drove his truck with the equipment and Wigwam took the Cadillac. After breakfast we were on our way.

Up 99 to I-80, turn right, head east for Reno, but get off in Colfax. Wigwam was so excited he missed the turn in Sacramento and was headed for San Francisco. The caravan soon corrected their mistake and were headed in the right direction. With little to no traffic, we were up the hill in no time, about 120 miles from Lodi. We were there. Just about eight A.M., we started to unload the truck and move the dredge, picks, shovels, pans, etc., down the road about half a mile, down a four-foot bank, and across the river rock, and the dredge equipment was launched.

The river, about a hundred feet wide, was right out of a Western movie, like *Paint Your Wagon*. It was quiet in some spots with a little current in the middle. As we looked up the river, we could see other dredges that were silent and covered from the night, the miners not yet up to turn them on for the day. We were the first miners of the day and we felt great.

As usual, Asshole donned his banana-colored wetsuit. Grizzly had purchased a new pair of Gabbelli's chest waders. Those two would man the dredge. River Rat quickly started the metal detector and started working the riverbanks. Sourdough and Wigwam started to hand-pan the old-fashioned way. There was no problem with the new pontoons, but the new nozzle took a couple of adjustments. We dredged and panned and detected for about five hours, emptying the dredge sluice box three times.

During the morning we noticed a miner who came in from behind us. He set up a high banker and ran a hose from the river. He just worked quietly with his pan and garden hand spade. He dug out of the banks a little at a time, and would take it back to his high banker and run it through. We didn't pay a whole lot of attention to him.

Towards noon he started to pack up and yelled out, "Hey guys, you can use my spot. I'm done for the day." We all went over to see how he had done and converse about his homemade high banker. He showed us his pan of the day's digs. It was amazing. He had more gold in that pan than the partners had ever seen. As soon as he left, River Rat, Sourdough, and Wigwam went to all the spots he had been in, filled a five-gallon bucket and ran it through our sluice.

It was one P.M. and Wigwam said it was time to start packing. We were all pretty tired and hot and had a ways to drive. We persuaded Grizzly and Asshole to float the dredge and a lot of the supplies downriver and we would pull them out next to the trucks. River Rat, Wigwam, and Sourdough packed out some stuff, while the dredge, Asshole, and Grizzly started downriver. Little did we know what lay in store.

The path back to the truck and cars veered away from the river and it wasn't until later that we realized that the elevation of the riverbank had changed. After the supplies were loaded on the truck, a miner from across the river yelled across to us, "Hey, did you lose a cooler?" We then knew there was trouble. As River Rat, Wigwam, and Sourdough headed back along the highest point of the trail, about 100 feet up from the river, we could see the yellow pontoons of the dredge beached up on land and Grizzly and Asshole gathering all the supplies they could find. Sourdough went down the cliff and found out what had happened.

Downriver from our panning site was some whitewater. The river narrowed and became deep, fast-running, and very rocky. It got too much for the partners to handle, but they didn't want to lose the rig, so they shot the rapids by hanging on to a rope. Grizzly later thought that Asshole was dead. They explained that it was more like rock surfing. Thank God both of the partners were okay. The pontoons filled with water due to a gash caused by a rock. The dredge had been so damaged that the unit had to be dismantled and hauled up the cliff by rope, one piece at a time.

Grizzly and Asshole had to change from their wet clothes. Grizzly had no problem, but Asshole always has trouble getting out of the banana suit. While Wigwam was tugging on the legs of the wetsuit, a bunch of girls started coming down the path. The miners took a tarp and held it up while the girls passed. I don't know what was worse, seeing Asshole in his underwear, or listening to the girls guessing what Wigwam and Asshole were doing behind the tarp. After about an hour, all the miners were in dry clothes, sipping a beer and resting up for the one-and-a-half-hour ride back to Lodi. Grizzly had a two-hour ride to Escalon.

We were all very tired, after a thirteen-hour day, 95 degrees in the hot sun, and two miners almost drowned, but we brought back over five gallons of the river's concentrate to be processed by hand during the next week. The partners were tired, but extremely happy. We felt that we had finally found the right spot. The team went home knowing that there was gold in the bucket, but just how much?

CHAPTER XXI

THE CLUBHOUSE

T he clubhouse is really Asshole's garage, remodeled into a workshop, with a kitchen, bathroom, and storage room in the back. It also has a cooler for the beer, cable TV, phones, a stereo (set only to the oldies station), and a half-dozen bar stools. The clubhouse is where we hold our board meetings every Wednesday, and conduct all of the business that normally comes before any board of directors.

At the workbench is where we process the gold, or should I say Asshole processes the gold. He painstakingly works a teaspoon of the concentrate at a time. Hand panning, outfitted with a headband and magnifying glass, Asshole spends hours working through the concentrates. The next Wednesday after the Bear River trip, all the partners were drooling to find out how much gold we had gotten, none of us really realizing how much effort and time it took on the part of our chairman.

River Rat made a motion to sell the trailer, as we have Grizzly's truck, and with the proceeds buy a desert fox or some other gold-separating machine. The motion carried, and the ad was placed in the local paper. Wigwam volunteered to come in and help pan out the concentrates the next day. Nine man-hours later, Asshole and Wigwam had only gone through about one inch of concentrate. This was unacceptable.

The next morning Wigwam picked up Asshole and headed for Auburn, to see Frank and Mindy at the Pioneer Mining Supplies Company. They had just what we were looking for, the blue dam bowl, patented by Frank twenty-some years ago, and it worked great. Wigwam got out the plastic and charged it, $237, which included an AC converter from Radio Shack. The partners would pay him back.

We were back at the clubhouse by noon, and Asshole was processing in fifteen minutes. This was Friday, and by Saturday Asshole was done. Did we find any gold? The answer is yes, not as much as we had hoped for, but more than we had ever gotten before, ever.

We know that the remainder of our expeditions this season will be back at the Bear River. It's the best gold-bearing location we have found.

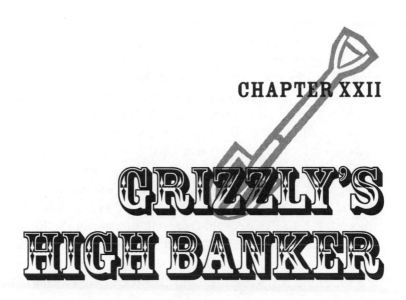

CHAPTER XXII

GRIZZLY'S HIGH BANKER

The next Wednesday the partners met for our regular board meeting. We were all very excited about the gold we had found and the new gold-separating machine that Asshole and Wigwam had purchased the previous Friday.

After the partners paid Wigwam back for the separating machine expenses, we started to discuss better ways to process and dig for gold. It then dawned on us that the guy who was mining behind us at Bear River was just walking around with a small hand spade and a bucket. He then ran his diggings through a high banker. When he left, all his mining supplies packed neatly into a wheelbarrow. One guy, one trip, and he didn't even break a sweat.

River Rat made a motion that we look into purchasing a high banker, so we pulled out the gold-mining supply catalogs and started looking them up. Wouldn't you know it, one model was about $850, and the cheapest was $480 without a pump.

Wigwam said, "Hey, Grizzly, you ought to be able to make one of those." Grizzly said, "Give me the picture," then said he would see what he could do. But what about the pump motor? Wigwam suggested that we get a bilge pump off a boat, like a big Chris Craft, and a marine battery. If Grizzly could put it together, it would be easier to pack in the high banker rather than the whole dredging rig, especially when all the partners can't go. The meeting adjourned, sending Grizzly on a mission to build a high banker.

The next week Grizzly showed up at the clubhouse with what looked like a green cat-litter box with a 24-inch sluice hanging out one end. It had PVC legs that screwed in, raising the height to about 18 inches on one end and 14 inches on the other. On the inside he had mounted PVC pipe. Around the pipe interior he drilled holes and mounted a hose spigot and control valve. He had also picked up a bilge pump and marine battery. The bill was under $125. But he had also bought a new valve to attach to the dredge motor, which would allow us to run the high banker off the dredge. So now we were able to run both units at the same time, keeping all the partners busy. But would it work? Grizzly had tested it at home and said he thought it would do the trick.

The partners were chomping at the bit to give it a try, but when could we all go? River Rat had to go to Chicago and Sourdough had to go down state on county business. So the retired miners, Asshole, Grizzly, and Wigwam, decided to go on a Wednesday. The best feature of Grizzly's high banker was that it would fold up and fit into the trunk of the Cadillac. This would make the trip up the hill a little nicer, with leather seats and Frank Sinatra CDs all the way.

CHAPTER XXIII

THE TEST

T he morning had finally come for the big test to see if Grizzly's high banker was going to work. Wigwam, like the rest of the miners, never slept the night before mining, due to the anticipation of the gold expedition and not wanting to oversleep and make everyone late.

This was the first mid-week trip for the partners, so there were new challenges to face—like getting through Sacramento before the morning rush hour, road repairs, closures, etc.

We decided that Grizzly would drive from Escalon and pick up Asshole by five A.M. in Stockton, then go to Wigwam's in Lodi. There they would load the Cadillac and head out for Colfax. The miners wanted to eat at George's in Lockford, but that was out of our way on this trip and nobody was real hot for stopping at Denny's. We decided to eat in Colfax and beat the traffic going to the capital.

Once the high banker and supplies were loaded, we were on our way. Colfax, here we come! It was a pleasant trip, with the miners conversing and getting caught up on any new developments in our lives since we had last seen each other.

We made it through Sacramento with no problems and started the ascent up Highway 80 towards Reno. As the sun broke through the mountain passes, it lit up the countryside and promised us a beautiful day. Once we reached our exit and turned off the highway, we started to look for a restaurant. Ed's Little Red Hen was not open, so we headed downtown and saw the lights on at Madonna's Restaurant, nestled in the middle of the block. As we entered, the waitress said, "Good morning. You guys can have some coffee, but we don't open till seven A.M." At exactly seven, she came and took our orders, and the food was just great.

Fueled up, we headed for the river, not far down the road. As we got closer to the river, seven deer jumped out into the road and stared at us, then leapt off the road and into the woods. To our surprise there was only one other vehicle at the side of the river. It looked like we would have the place all to ourselves.

Asshole grabbed the high banker and Grizzly and Wigwam took turns carrying the battery and buckets. We headed down to our spot on the river. The morning sun was just starting to sparkle on the river as we set up the high banker. Some turkey buzzards were roosting in a tree, and an osprey flew straight down the river, looking for a nice fish for breakfast.

We were ready for the test. We gave Grizzly the honors of turning on the switch. Once the machine was started, the water began flowing and it worked perfectly. Grizzly was quite proud and I was proud of him.

Asshole decided to walk down the river and check it out. While he was gone, Grizzly and Wigwam dug around the roots of a dead tree and around the crevices of some boulders nearby. We had talked and worked for only about forty-five minutes when Asshole returned. He said that there were sixteen dredging units set up all along the river. This was really the spot.

As the test was finished, we gathered the concentrate and headed for the car. This was a breeze compared to the dredge operation. Loaded up, we headed up towards the dam to see if there were any other accesses to the river, but there were none.

Reaching the bridge at Highway 174, we got out and Grizzly took some pictures. We saw a sign for a campground at Rollins Lake in Nevada County. We checked it out—nice campground, hot showers, and only five miles from our river. We agreed to camp out on our next trip. On our way out of the camp we saw about four wild turkeys grazing at the side of the road.

We had told the other partners to meet us at the clubhouse about four P.M., when we would process the test concentrates through the gold separator and have a regular meeting. Having some time to spare, we took old Highway 49 the entire way back to enjoy the countryside and the company.

We got back to the clubhouse right on time, set up the blue dam bowl and started the processing: first the hundred mesh, then sieve through the fifty mesh and the final sieve, thirty mesh. Asshole started to feed the concentrates into the bowl and there they were: over forty-five pieces of gold just lying there, sparkling and glowing!

This was a great success, for all the partners, Grizzly's high banker, the dredge, the river, and the gold. It was all coming together. We decided to make another trip the next Wednesday. Asshole, Grizzly, and Wigwam headed back up the hill. After three hours of digging and using the high banker, we had over three hundred pieces of gold.

The only downside is that this is now October and the dredge season will be over on the fifteenth. But we will be ready for next season.

CHAPTER XXII

ANNUAL REPORT

All publicly traded companies and any business worth its salt will take time to reflect on the year's successes and failures and report such to its shareholders and/or principal owners. The findings are:

The C.S.O., formerly known as the Chicken Shit Outfit, is alive and well. Although expenses have exceeded revenues, this was primarily due to capital investments made to enhance and improve our mining operations and processing facilities.

Additionally, research and development costs were abnormally high due to the extensive search for the right gold-bearing fields. The company officers feel that our next season will meet and/or exceed analyst estimates.

More importantly, the company's management team is committed to this company, its goals and its vision for the future.

In summary, the miners associated with the C.S.O. have not only become professional, but are dedicated to each other. They have total trust in each other. They have stood by each other in the field, they have worked together as a team and they have shared the disappointments, which has made them stronger and more determined to succeed.

Many companies spend hundreds of thousands of dollars annually to motivate and teach their executive management teams, through survival courses, to trust in their team members, knowing they won't let you down. If the C.S.O. finds no other gold, the real gold is in the friendships that have been formed, which will be everlasting.

The search will continue!

ABOUT THE AUTHOR

Edward L. Allum has just completed a 28-year career as a health-care administrator, retiring in April 2000 from San Joaquin County General Hospital. He is a graduate of Michigan's Andrews University, Food Service Administrators Certificate Program, and the Lake Superior State University Health Care Manager Development Program. He is an experienced executive, specializing in multi-department and multi-unit management, and has been highly successful in personnel training, development, and current motivational techniques.

Edward has received many awards. Those of which he is most proud include Employer of the Year—1996, received from the Private Industry Council/Right Track in support of disadvantaged youth; and Health Care Manager of the Year—1989. Edward has been providing consultant services to hospitals across the country for many years. Edward and his wife reside in California, near the Mother Lode region and Gold Country.

Books Available from Robert D. Reed Publishers

Please include payment with orders. Send indicated book(s) to:

Name:_____

Address:_____

City/State/Zip:_____

Phone:(_____)_____ E-mail:_____

No.	Titles and Authors	Unit Price
____	*The Fiddletown Journal: Stories of the Mother Lode* by Edward L. Allum	$9.95
____	*Gotta Minute? 50 Tips for Organizing Your Life!* by Irene Lawrence	7.95
____	*Gotta Minute? Practical Tips for Abundant Living: The ABC's of Total Health* by Tom Massey, Ph.D., M.D.	9.95
____	*Gotta Minute? Yoga for Health, Relaxation & Well-Being* by Nirvair Singh Khalsa	9.95
____	*Gotta Minute? How to Look and Feel Great!* by Marcia F. Kamph, M.S., D.C.	11.95
____	*Gotta Minute? Ultimate Guide of One-Minute Workouts for Anyone, Anywhere, Anytime!* by Bonnie Nygard, M.Ed. & Bonnie Hopper, M.Ed.	9.95
____	*A Kid's Herb Book for Children of All Ages* by Lesley Tierra, Acupuncturist and Herbalist	19.95
____	*Saving the Soul of Medicine* by M. A. Mahony, M.D.	21.95

No.	Titles and Authors	Unit Price
____	*House Calls: How We Can All Heal the World One Visit at a Time* by Patch Adams, M.D.	11.95
____	*500 Tips for Coping with Chronic Illness* by Pamela D. Jacobs, M.A.	11.95

Enclose a photocopy of this order form with payment for books. Send to the address below.

Shipping & handling: $2.50 for first book plus $1.00 for each additional book.

California residents add 8.5% sales tax.

We offer discounts for large orders.

Please make checks payable to the publisher: Robert D. Reed.

Total enclosed: $_____. See our website for more books!

Robert D. Reed Publishers
750 La Playa, Suite 647, San Francisco, CA 94121
Phone: (650) 994-6570 • Fax: (650) 994-6579
Email: 4bobreed@msn.com • www.rdrpublishers.com